T'shuvah

Richard Jeffrey Newman

Fernwood
PRESS

T'shuvah

©2023 Richard Jeffrey Newman

Fernwood Press
Newberg, Oregon
www.fernwoodpress.com

All rights reserved. No part may be reproduced
for any commercial purpose by any method without
permission in writing from the copyright holder.

Printed in the United States of America

Page layout: Mareesa Fawver Moss
Cover photo: Ante Gudelj via unsplash.com
Author photo: Brian T. Silak Photography | briansilakphotography.com

ISBN 978-1-59498-112-8

For Adam Schonbrun (ז״ל), who knew what it meant to earn,
and to fail to earn, the laughter this book ends with.

Table of Contents

Acknowledgments 7
Author's Note 9
Yom Kippur 5780 13
Do Not Wish For Any Other Life 29
Insomnia 39
   What Will Not Let Itself Be Washed Away 40
   A Dream in Three Parts 43
   Just Beyond Your Reach 46
   Insomnia 47
This Sentence Is a Metaphor for Bridge 49
Notes 71
First Line Index 73

Acknowledgments

Thank you to the following journals and publications in which some of these poems appeared:

> *Unlikely Stories:* "What Will Not Let Itself Be Washed Away" and "Do Not Wish For Any Other Life" (in an earlier version as "Four Variations and a Theme")
> *iamb:* "Just Beyond Your Reach"
> *BigCityLit:* "A Dream in Three Parts"

Some sections of "This Sentence Is a Metaphor for Bridge" were published in earlier versions and with different numbering in the following publications:

> *The Piltdown Review:* #3, #4, #12, and #16
> *Birds Fall Silent in the Mechanical Sea* (Great Weather for Media 2019): #13
> *BigCityLit:* #6, #15, #20
> *Open: Journal of Arts & Letters:* #18

Author's Note

T'shuvah (Hebrew, תשובה) means repentance or atonement. Etymologically, it comes from the root meaning "to return," and it names the central component of repentance within Judaism. The logic, as I learned it when I was in yeshiva, goes like this: if sin alienates you from your authentic, spiritual, and God-fearing self, then the way to atone for sin is to return to that self as a starting point from which to deepen your commitment to the life God wants you to lead. The poems in *T'shuvah* apply this framing to the question of how one "returns" from the alienation that is inherent in surviving sexual violence, with the caveat, of course, that a survivor of sexual violence has committed no sin and that neither the moralizing nature nor the implicit politics of the phrase "the life God wants you to lead" need by definition to be part of anyone's return/healing.

כל העולם כולו גשר צר מאוד, והעיקר - לא לפחד כלל

Kol ha'olam kulo gesher tzar me'od, veha'ikar lo le'fached klal.

All the world is a very narrow bridge, and the most important thing is not to be overwhelmed by fear.

—Rabbi Nachman of Breslov

Yom Kippur 5780

On Yom Kippur 5780, October 9, 2019, a heavily armed gunman, shouting that Jews were "the root" of "problems" such as feminism and mass immigration, tried to shoot his way into a synagogue in Halle, Germany. When he did not succeed, he shot and killed two people nearby.

1

Black cat in the browning grass
at the base of the red brick wall
as you turn the corner at 77th Street,
its yellow eyes taking the measure
of the danger you represent
despite the fence you'd have to leap
to get to it, and the slow,
inscrutable turn of its head
tracking each step you take
as you walk past, ear buds in,
Philip Glass's "Symphony No. 8"
turned up loud enough
that you don't notice,
till you're almost on the other side
of where he's sitting,
the elderly Sikh, orange dastār,
wispy white beard, one hand
wrapped around the top of his cane,
tensing as if he intends to rise
to make sure you receive
before you're too far away to hear
the morning greeting
he's calling out,

but he lifts his other hand instead,
and from the bottom steps
of the staircase leading
to the second story door
of the two-family house
you assume is his home,

he waves, and that's
when the recognition glimmering
beneath his arched eyebrows
and in his smile
registers, so you raise
your own hand and smile back,
just as you've done
almost every day since you began
these pre-dawn walks
your doctor prescribed,

except your friend is usually perched
on the low wall at the corner of 73rd Street,
edge of the Lexington School for the Deaf's
schoolyard, his back not quite touching
the chain links behind him; his hands
flat against the concrete on either side;
that same cane resting between his legs,
curved handle pointing
to the middle of his chest;
his eyes closed, and yet—
maybe the music you walk to
announces your presence—
he always somehow
turns his wide face toward you
the moment you cross the street,
raises his hand as he's just done,
and smiles, returning
to the world behind his eyelids
the moment your own greeting is complete,

but this time, as you keep pace
with the eighth-note pulse
of Glass's strings,
you feel him focus on your face
a vigilance that makes you nervous,
so you force yourself not to look back
as you turn right onto 25th Avenue,
and I wonder, as you leave his line of sight,
if you feel my scrutiny as well,
because I too am watching,
sitting here this Yom Kippur morning,
as the path you weave
back and forth
across this page
revises the mental map
I hold in my head
of my own early-AM treks,

which is not the metaphor
I started these lines to plumb,
but then you, the second person,
flowed so naturally into their rhythm
that I chose you
without even realizing I'd chosen.

2

As if choosing to write on this day,
even after three decades
of not setting foot in shul,
of eating whatever I want
whenever I want, of trying to live
as if repentance required nothing—no,
as if nothing I've done
requires repentance—no,
as if I'd left at last behind
the all-knowing bookkeeper god
for whom repentance settles
all accounts—no, as if
Rabbi Wahrman's voice
from 11th grade gemara class,
deep and wide enough
that I sometimes lost myself
in the cadence of his learning,
does not still come to me, as if
he never looked out at our class,
eyes filled with a father's love,
pleading with us—we
were his wayward children—
"If you take honest stock,
you'll know the truth.
The yiddisheh neshama
you couldn't disown if you tried
yearns for HaShem. Don't
get in its way!"

               As if all of that
and none of that, I am here,
following you past the Bulova Corporate Center
till the avenue opens out
onto a treeless field of grass
you've never seen.
I watch as you realize
you don't know where you are,
as you start turning in circles,
searching for a landmark—
the familiar shape
of a house or a streetlamp
or the playground that should still be visible
two blocks behind you to your left—
but there is nothing, not even
the street you start to doubt was ever there,
and *that's* when you look up, sensing
what you would not call my presence
because you do not know it's me,
but it's me, and you freeze,
feline-ready to bolt,
because the reflex in you
that kicks in whenever
escape feels necessary
kicks in,
just like Adam
in the Garden of Eden,

whom you are not,
as I am not
God pretending
I don't already know
where you're hiding,
because you're not hiding,
there's nothing for you to hide behind,
and you are not naked
or newly ashamed to know you're naked,
so you start walking again—
you've no idea what else to do—
and the field becomes a path
so wide you cannot stray,
the horizon you're heading for
always straight ahead,
no matter which direction you choose.

3

You start singing along as loud as you can
to Marc Cohn's "Walk Through The World,"
hoping his words will conjure,
not the final point you need to reach
but the life you need to move through to get there,
and that's when you step
into Tibbets Brook Park,
where Maryam and I always stop
to sit by the lake with our bikes,
except you're by yourself,
standing beneath a willow
where two red-winged blackbirds,
one near the top, the other
on a branch directly over your head,
sing for mates you hope they find.

You're watching a large German shepherd
amble toward you,
oblivious it seems
to the white woman calling him
back to where she's waiting,
one hand on the handle
of an old-fashioned green baby carriage,
the other on the shoulder
of the tallest of three small girls
arrayed in front of her,
each a different hue,
though none match hers.

The shepherd's snout
against your palm
demands attention.
You curl your fingers
into the fur behind his left ear,
but then the summons he knows
he must ultimately answer—
"Samson! Come here, boy!"—
becomes more compelling
than his curiosity,
and he trots off as if you'd never been there,
sits obedient beside the stroller
while the shortest of the three girls
puts on him the collar and leash
she's been holding out like a treat.

4

At precisely that moment,
another dog shoots past,
large and white,
drops of water
flying off his fur,
chasing two dark-skinned boys on scooters,
who stop at the bottom of the hill,
twisting their necks to see if he's kept up,
but he stops too,
barks once in their direction
and races back to the hill's crest,
where he puts his front paws
on the chest of the man
who obviously gave those boys
their eyes and noses;

and you're remembering
how Jake barked just like that
every time Shahob ran
what was about to become
too far ahead; and how we lied
when Jake slipped his leash
and the car that did not stop
somehow did not kill him—how we lied
so our boy would not have to know
that because the death the vet
assured us he could not stop
was not coming fast enough,
the only true mercy
was to let him kill our pet.

5

Unlike Mikey, who wasn't dying
when I got down with him
on his vet's blue tarp,
but that memory is not for you,
at least not yet,
so you turn left out of the park,
onto the mountain trail in Darakeh,
where your brother-in-law used to live.
You pass a couple
loading plastic grocery bags
onto a white pack mule,
the bell hanging over its forehead
ringing not ten minutes later
for you to move aside,
which you do, almost tripping
over the loose stones
lining the trail's edge. The man
on the mule's back grins,
calls out, "So-rry!"
and steers his ride down a path
steeper than you'd trust
any animal to carry you,
and not a single bag falls,
not one apple tumbles
from the bagful you saw his wife
hang last from the saddle.

You start to follow anyway,
but your first step lands you
in the mosque-that-is-also-an-entrance
to Tehran's bazaar:
long shadows crisscrossing
the black-and-white
mosaicked marble floor,
a fountain in the corner,
cups at the edge
for washing before prayers.

You walk through that place of worship
into a network of alleyways
lined on either side
with merchants selling everything
from carpets to underwear.
A motorcycle weaves
slowly toward you
through the crowd.
In the driver's lap,
a goat, gray and black,
someone's dinner perhaps,
struggles to free itself.
"Agha, bepah!" the driver calls out,
as Maryam pulls you to the side—

6

—and you're stepping through the door at Thanksgiving,
the aunts and uncles drunk, the cousins
doing shots of Patrón in the kitchen.
The one who said he'd meet
any woman his family arranged
except a Jewish one
holds out the shot that could be yours,
and you do not hesitate,
choose the backdoor instead,
face once more
the edge of the field that shouldn't be there,
where it is still the Day of Atonement,
and Rabbi Wahrman's voice is still in your ears,
"Done right, t'shuvah means
returning not to where you were,
because that's where you went astray,
but to where you should have been all along."

In the news today from Germany,
yet one more white man with a gun—
though they are not always white,
and they don't always use guns—
launched himself against a synagogue.
This time, no Jews were murdered.

"T'shuvah," Reb Wahrman would've said,
"is itself a shield," and if one of us had asked
about the Jews massacred in Pittsburgh
or the woman who gave her life in Poway
to save her rabbi, Reb Wahrman
would have responded,

"HaKadosh-Boruch-Hoo has His reasons.
Who are we to question them?"

You turn from those words just as I did,
determined to keep faith only with yourself,
but a stone wall higher than you can see to the top of
blocks your way, the narrow door
open directly in front of you
your only invitation forward.

I don't know why you do not panic
when the latch clicks shut behind you,
but you move through that space
in which you suddenly cannot see
the hand you lift to rub your eyes with
like it's the last time you'll walk
through a much-loved home.

Then the floor begins to crumble,
and the walls, and through the cracks
opening in the ceiling
light starts seeping in,
each bit of brightness
a stone you step on
to stay above the surface of the dark.

Do Not Wish For Any Other Life

1

What hangs around your neck will not take wing.
What closes like a fist around your heart
will never keep you safe. Pick up your pen.
Refuse the comfort of your own white skin.

2

Embrace those broken wings; forgo the clouds.
The time for patience and restraint has passed,
so leave aside the mercies you've received.
There is no suppurating wound to hide.
Your hunger will dissolve what doesn't burn.

3

You chose disbelief and lived bereft,
so offer what you dare against the wind.
Metaphors cost what love's last kiss redeems.

4

This landscape gravitates toward gratitude.
This page embraces what defiles it.
Edges bleed where other edges meet them.

5

The failed dishonesty you call your lust
lives in the hollow carved out by your guilt.

Let laughter be desire's winding shroud.
Pronounce *vagina* like a libertine.

6

Force a fledgling's language from your mouth.
Pry open the long crease where shame settles.
Console yourself that fear is a god's first gift.

7

The past you grieve will rise. Wrap your tongue
around its root and pull. What draws you forward
through the faith you've lost will not desert you.
Interrogate the love it implicates.
What leaves the body leaves itself behind.

8

Here, at least, you know what you know is true.
The snow's indifference will not repay your debt,
but do not wish for any other life.
You must not wish for any other life!

Insomnia

What Will Not Let Itself Be Washed Away

On that boy's night out in Jamshil thirty years ago,
in the song-in disco at the far end of Saemaeul Shijang,
the dancer your friends insisted you had to see
stepped when the applause stopped
down from the stage
and paraded herself naked
around the room, pouring drinks
for the men but not the women
watching from the tables
lining the dance floor.

When she reached the spot
where you were seated,
her eyes widened—your white face
was not a common sight back then—
and she shimmied past the knees
of the two men sitting to your left,
who did not touch her as she passed,
to curl naked in your lap.
She filled your soju shot glass
precisely to the brim, without a word
opened her thighs wide enough
to press your fingers flat
to where you'd have to pay to enter,
and held them there
with a firmness you chose
not to resist.

Then she shimmied back out
to join the man waiting at the door,
holding out for her the robe she wore

when she first strutted into the spotlight,
but before she turned her back on you forever,
she plucked a rose from the centerpiece,
fixed her gaze to yours,
and tucked the flower
neatly into your breast pocket,
a blossom you kept
in a window-sill-soda-bottle vase
till only the stem remained.

Tonight, your skin a solitude
you cannot wash away,
you want to feel again
the moment of that giving,
so you lift your tumbler—
scotch you've been nursing since 8:30—
and toast the two of them,
dancer and handler,
as he drapes the robe
over her shoulder
and she walks out ahead of him,
eyes focused nowhere but forward.

In second grade,
a girl whose name
you want to say was Rachel
walked with you every day
halfway home from school.
As if on cue, at the corner
where she turned left
and you turned right,

she always turned
her large and hazel eyes
to you, waiting
for you to say goodbye first.

Once, in spring,
a rhythm entered you
and you found words
you wish you could remember.
They were perfect,
meant *I love you,*
but then the girl is gone,
and nothing you have written
has ever brought her back.

A Dream in Three Parts

1

The girl who turned her back on you
when you were twelve
to be a girl who gave herself to fashion
returns to offer you her hips.
She peels from perfect porcelain skin
the same shade of pink she wore
the last time you saw her in shul,
and you fuck as if you're dueling,
sinking into each other
over and over again
the well-honed blades
of dismissed compassion.

Tell your *children lies if you must!*
she whispers through clenched teeth,
first beneath you, then with her face
inches above yours, her nails
pushing each syllable
into your chest.
*These trysts with ghosts
are yours to keep,
not theirs.*

2

A pregnant white woman
wheels her daughter
through the heavy double doors,
parks the stroller in the front row,
and waddles up onto the bimah.

The child, mouth half-open,
tongue a tiny spear between her lips,
pushes hard to taste the world
beyond the restraints
holding her in place.

She stops, looks straight at you,
calls your name, her voice
the voice your father used
when he bought you back from God
for five silver dollars. *Is this
your mother's true desire?*

The question yanks your dreaming-self awake.

3

When you close your eyes again,
the room is the same,
but the girl, still restrained,
is crying. Her mother,
leaning down to comfort her,
doesn't see that you've returned.

In blue jeans worn thin at the knees
and a pristine but untucked
white tee shirt, the fashion model
beckons from the door through which
when you were friends
you'd escape the rabbi's sermons
to play in the all-purpose room downstairs.

Standing equidistant from each woman,
naked and somehow unburnt,
your clothes a pile of ash at your feet,
you raise your pistol.

You should have understood
the task that brought you here
would be other than the obvious.

Just Beyond Your Reach

The prayer you say is neither seed nor plow,
nor is it rain to quench your soul's old thirst.
The parched and blistered field your tongue is now
bespeaks the long neglect about to burst,
like rotten fruit thrown to chase from the stage
a comic leaving dead words at your feet;
and she, or maybe he, responds with rage,
shrinking the room until the single seat
that's left is where you're planted. Confront your god,
shimmering and luscious, there, his skin—
or is it hers?—a proffered gift, a prod
to every hunger you have called a sin.

Welcome each new taste; spread wide; bow low.
Lose yourself till loss is all you know.

Insomnia

It isn't just the clock that measures time.
The earth is moving darkness overhead.
Or darkness doesn't move; then you're dead.
Stealing someone's minutes is a crime.
The words tonight are bound in perfect rhyme,
but rhythm falters in this dullness spread
like stones across your chest. Your breath is lead;
your flesh, a pale and impotent paradigm.

The nakedness you fear is no one's hell.
Love makes everyone an infidel.

This Sentence Is
a Metaphor for Bridge

1

Take refuge on this path
the page gives you to roam.

Hunker down against
the shadow cast by prayer
and build yourself a line
that won't efface itself.

Language is not wine.
You cannot pour it freely.

2

Beneath each step you take,
the chiseled wisdom
stone cannot refuse.

Beyond the edge of reprimand,
where faith insists you wait,
white and voiceless,
for blame to fall from the clouds,
the road remembers
every promise you have kept.

It will repay you
what you're owed.

3

The dreams that leave you stranded
on a ledge you hope you will not die on
don't negate the ones
you run naked through,
bright as a waxing crescent
slitting darkness open.

Face your shame.
Then sweep the air
above your head
with flame.

4

Like endless tea leaves
in a paper cup,
the words swirling
in your unshod brain
refuse to come to rest.

Undo the ligatures
binding your name.
You will not burn,
nor will the earth beneath you
cease to turn,
if you embrace
this fallow field,
this barefoot love
you're here to render.

5

You cannot know
before it happens
what comes next,
cannot give away
the vast expanse
you're heir to. Forget
how long you hid. Reject
the splintered ethics
that would buy your silence.
Your path is clear.
There is no balance
without fear.

6

Before you have a chance
to sing a word,
the music stops,
its final note
a pebble dropped
from high above the trees.

The ripple spreads itself
along the path you use
to steer your herd toward home.
Forget the wood you've chopped.
Alone, you'll never build
the necessary fire,
and in this metaphor,
you *are* alone. So place
that sharpened stone
before the altar,
watch the light approach,
and tell us what you see.

What you perceive
is pointless obfuscation.

7

Between each breath
they tried to make you pay,
the coin you failed to spend;
between each spin
they let you give the wheel,
a naked lover
weeping in your lap.

The blood-red flowers
you mistook for sacrifice
redeemed nothing.
You hoarded failure,
hoped the heaven
you'd been promised
would be waiting.

Your tongue is a trembling leaf
barely holding on
before the coming storm.
Make yourself what love obliterates.
You've chased forgiveness long enough.

8

You watch the men and women on the screen
fuck and suck each other without sound,
without regard for orifice or gender.
You want to touch them where the wind cannot,
to pull aside the veil and free their grief.

Proud that you have not demeaned the risk
this witnessing demands, you hope the tale
that will be yours when they, and you, are done,
will pull at last your swollen anger shut.

You live for the choice to give or kill this pleasure.
The pleasure lives as long as you don't choose.

9

Now that you've confessed,
speak no word aloud.
Turn to face the pit
and watch the cloudless sky
this day has granted you
refuse to darken.

Released from their branches,
autumn leaves drift down,
yellow, red, orange,
some still green,
to rest at your feet.

Like your prayers,
they will not rise again,
but don't confuse surrender
with defeat. Ride instead
this curve of language
like water down the face of a cliff;
put the lips of this imagined form made real
to the mouth of what you've marred
and breathe. The world
invites you only once
to be its bride.
Nothing you regret
hurts more than that.

10

Put on your whitest smock
and use those bloodstained sheets
to spin a tale you will not have to smooth.

You cannot circumvent
the death curled naked at your feet,
cannot refuse the chaos you require
the room it needs to grow.

Redeem the hunger you've survived.
Force yourself to watch
as if a fallen hope
could fill your empty hands.

11

The dead inhabit every step you take.
They grope the dark,
the heft of wanting
and wanting not to understand,
bending their backs
as if the weight were real.

Do not think of this as hope.
No matter how much noise they make,
the dead weigh nothing.

12

You counted them
before you understood
that you were counting,
wrapped each one
in a scrap of newsprint,
and placed them side-by-side
in the basket your neighbor
left at your door
with the shoes you once said
looked comfortable enough
to walk a hundred miles in.
You tied those laces tight.

Let the rotting corpses
you have borne here
settle in the dust.
Honor the rift.
If you plan to stay,
shed everything that's not a gift.

13

This trespass into verse
will not prepare you;
nor will you find
the strength you'll need
beneath that willow's bend.

The silver wren
singing to its mate
on the bare branch
above the river—
root your resistance there.

The snow will grace the ground beneath your feet
like fine lace on a wedding gown,
but nothing white survives the mud.
Reject the faith they tempt you with:
that day must fill its night
with dreams of failed escape,
that *you* will fail,
that failure whites out rape.

14

When the god-who-isn't
returns to enter you,
and the river you skipped stones across
when you were hairless and untouched
becomes the past you want
but cannot have,
reconcile what you can.

You've never been
the gazelle the cheetah
can't bring down,
have failed at willing
caged doves into flight.
The tongues you've taken
between your lips
have never pulsed
with the heat of the days
you've yet to live.

Deceit begins when touch fails,
when hunger becomes an argument.

15

Unhook what's stretched across your ribs,
part ways
with the memory of silk,
and remember how you learned
what not to swallow,
the drops you hid
beneath your tongue.

The rage you've borne till now
has readied you for this.
Give your heart the room it needs.
Leave the comfort of your skin behind.

16

We're here because we trust that you won't leave,
because these fallen leaves distort death's face,
because what fell from you is less reprieve
than simple logic falling into place.

The future forms in increments of sound,
the footsteps of those fingers on your thigh.
What rises overflows its banks. Unbound,
it grows until it fills the evening sky.

It's more than rhythm calls these words to form.
It's more than precedent.

You've come this far to learn what love's about.
So turn it over; see what rattles out.

17

When you arrived,
faith pounced,
a mother lion
with cubs to feed,
and you made yourself food,
rising from the muck
of your survival—
the scrape and grovel,
the whining, the rage—
to offer freely
all the small prosperities
you no longer needed;

and when you stood before us,
a child newly bathed,
and there was no shame,
then you knew
that what you knew
was true, and the path
you took to get here,
the agony and doubt
each step forced you to endure,
receded into silence.

That's when you were warned,
as we all have been,

but when your time came,
you convinced yourself
love glistened the tip
of every word your seducer spoke.
You split yourself in two.

Now one of you—
and you will have to choose—
must die. We, of course,
will welcome home
whichever one survives.

18

Strap betrayal's instrument
tight around your waist.
Wear like armor
the narrow grief
you practice in your dreams.

The one way in
remains the one way in.
What providence is not
is not to blame.

19

Waiting is also
a road for you to travel,
a mirror you don't dare deface,
so before you ask
whose bridge this is,
picture a guard dog
pulling tight
a rusted chain
bolted to the deck
just past the abutment.

The conflict ends
when one of you releases seeds.

20

Imagine Gehinnom unfenced,
yourself the unburned center
of all that burning,
every prayer you've ever said
undone line by line,
until the empty page
is all you have.

Enter there the path in you
that is only a path,
gather its shadows
into a dance,
a movement
that ends with love,
that keeps on moving
till love becomes the rhythm,
and you the fire, and the dance,
the life you've chosen
to make your loving possible.

You thought you had to be
the clench you've held
where none but you
could feel it.

Give yourself instead
to all that rises.
Fill that cloudless sky
with laughter.

Notes

Yom Kippur 5780: *Shul,* synagogue. *Yiddishe neshama,* Jewish soul. *HaShem,* literally "The Name," the term religious Jews use for God when they are not praying or reading from the Torah, a way to make sure not to say God's name in vain. *Darakeh,* a neighborhood in the north of Tehran. *Agha, bepah,* "Sir, get out of the way!" *HaKadosh-Boruch-Hoo,* a name for God, literally "The Holy One, Blessed Be He."

Do Not Wish For Any Other Life: *What hangs around your neck will not take wing* is a reference to the albatross in Samuel Taylor Coleridge's "The Rime of the Ancient Mariner."

What Will Not Let Itself Be Washed Away: *Jamshil,* an area of Seoul. *Song-in disco,* a term that may no longer be in use for an "adult disco," one which hosted erotic performances and at which paid female companionship was available. *Saemaeul Shijang,* a market in Jamshil.

The Task That Brought You Here: *When he bought you back from God...* This refers to the Jewish ceremony known as pidyon haben, redemption of the first-born. In Exodus (13:12–15), the Israelites are instructed to set aside all first-born male creatures for God, but they are also instructed to redeem all first-born sons. The cost of redemption is set in Numbers (18:15–16) as five silver shekels, which Jews in the United States who observe this tradition have translated to five silver dollars.

This Sentence Is a Metaphor for Bridge, #20: *Gehinnom,* the name for the Jewish version of hell, which is not a place of eternal damnation. Rather, it is broadly understood to be a place where one's soul is purified in preparation for its entry into heaven and God's presence. In some versions, fire is the means by which this purification takes place.

First Line Index

Symbols
   —and you're stepping through
   the door at Thanksgiving 26

A
   A pregnant white woman 44
   As if choosing to write on this day 18
   At precisely that moment 23

B
   Before you have a chance 55
   Beneath each step you take 51
   Between each breath 56
   Black cat in the browning grass 15

E
   Embrace those broken wings; forgo the clouds 31

F
   Force a fledgling's language from your mouth 35

H

Here, at least, you know what you know is true 37

I

Imagine Gehinnom unfenced 70
It isn't just the clock that measures time 47

L

Like endless tea leaves 53

N

Now that you've confessed 58

O

On that boy's night out in Jamshil thirty years ago 40

P

Put on your whitest smock 59

S

Strap betrayal's instrument 68

T

Take refuge on this path 50
The dead inhabit every step you take 60
The dreams that leave you stranded 52
The failed dishonesty you call your lust 34
The girl who turned her back on you 43
The past you grieve will rise. Wrap your tongue 36
The prayer you say is neither seed nor plow 46
This landscape gravitates toward gratitude 33
This trespass into verse 62

U

Unhook what's stretched across your ribs 64
Unlike Mikey, who wasn't dying 24

W

Waiting is also 69
We're here because we trust that you won't leave 65
What hangs around your neck will not take wing 30
When the god-who-isn't 63
When you arrived 66
When you close your eyes again 45

Y

You cannot know 54
You chose disbelief and lived bereft 32
You counted them 61
You start singing along as loud as you can 21
You watch the men and women on the screen 57

www.ingramcontent.com/pod-product-compliance
Lightning Source LLC
Chambersburg PA
CBHW011344090426
42743CB00019B/3434